OZZY MAN'S

MAD WORLD

First published in 2017

Text copyright © Ozzy Man Studios Pty Ltd, 2017

Photographs have been reproduced in this book for the express
purpose of parody and satire.

Allen & Unwin
83 Alexander Street
Crows Nest NSW 2065
Australia

Phone: (61 2) 8425 0100
Email: info@allenandunwin.com
Web: www.allenandunwin.com

Cataloguing-in-Publication details are available from the National Library
of Australia www.trove.nla.gov.au

ISBN 978 1 76063 118 5

Internal design by Hugh Ford
Photographs of Ozzy Man by Daniel Ahmadi
danielahmadiphotography.com
Printed in Australia by Australian Book Connection

10 9 8 7 6 5 4 3 2 1

OZZY MAN'S

MAD WORLD

A COLLECTION OF THE GREATEST WTF MOMENTS ON EARTH (SO FAR)

ALLEN&UNWIN

SYDNEY · MELBOURNE · AUCKLAND · LONDON

CONTENTS

INTRODUCTION

The purpose of this fancy book can be summarised like a PowerPoint presentation.

Purpose:
1) To personally collate 30 of my favourite video commentaries and display them to ya in the age-old book format. It's a collection of Ozzy Man's best times to date.

2) To provide ya with further written commentary on the videos and to give ya some behind-the-scenes stories!

Throughout the book you'll notice pages titled 'OZZY MAN REFLECTS'. Those are the sections where shit gets meta. You could say it's where Ozzy Man reviews . . . Ozzy Man. Anyhow, I'm getting too psychedelic on ya now. Don't mind me.

Overall, this book is a collectible and a reflection. I fair dinkum hope you'll gain some level of entertainment out of it. I also hope you hear my voice in your head as you read it. Feel free to use any of ya favourite one-liners from the commentaries in a toast at a distinguished event, or if you go to hospital soon and a nurse asks you what level of pain you're feeling you can say, 'DESTINATION FUCKED! is the level I'm at, thank you.' Use 'em wherever and whenever ya like.

Cheers!

Ozzy Man

Ozzy Man Reviews
ICE-BUCKET
CHALLENGE FAILS

Released: 20 August 2014 on YouTube and Facebook

'She fucken stacks it from shit footwear! In runs the other fruit loop and pours the bucket over both of them. Two girls, one bucket, a fuckload of screaming.'

'Everyone pictured here looks massively under-confident, which is the best time to try new things.'

I AM TRYING TO FIGUREOUT HOW HUMANS HAVE MADE IT [...] WAY TO 2017!

'Fuck me dead, how can being drunk and dressed as Mario possibly end well?'

'Here she goes, hoists it up, misses, but acts like she did it anyway.'

'Oh fantastic, another attempt from a great height and an instant knockout.'

OZZY MAN REFLECTS ...

What I love about the ice-bucket challenge videos is how poorly most people making them thought shit out. It always seemed like a simple challenge . . . but a lot could go wrong, and thankfully for all of us everyday internet users a lot *did* go wrong and people filmed it. Ice blocks were too cold, the ground was too slippery, the water was too heavy, and egos went through the roof as everyone tried pouring bigger buckets or dropping them from greater heights.

After I finished my first-ever videos on *Game of Thrones*, I was wondering what the hell I could tackle next. Online trends seemed to have the perfect amount of chaos for an Ozzy Man review. I can't be that cynical towards online trends but, as ridiculous as some of 'em appear to be, they can do good in the world. The ALS Ice Bucket Challenge raised around 115 million bucks for the ALS Association, according to bloody *Forbes* and *Time* (I googled that shit). I can't be that cynical towards people partaking in a silly idea that raises money for charity. I'm happy to remain cynical at how that money is distributed and spent after everyone has done the work to raise it, though. Hopefully it has not been wasted!

Since the ice-bucket challenge, we've also seen trends such as the condom challenge, bottle flipping, the mannequin challenge, the floor is lava game, and the corn drill challenge (that shit was fucked up). There wasn't a charity aspect to those ones, but that didn't stop huge numbers of people from getting involved in stupid shit.

Call me old school, but I personally enjoy trends like yo-yos, Tamagotchis and Tazos.

Source videos, from start of section: (1) The Besties Show, Nicole Marie Johnson and Carrie Finkley; (2) Sofie Tollefson and Jukin Video; (3) John Deluca and Collab Clips; (4) source unknown; (5) Launchpad Screeners; (6, 7) Grady Riley and Jukin Video

Ozzy Man Reviews
NICKI MINAJ, 'ANACONDA'
Released: 24 August 2014 on YouTube and Facebook

'The anaconda has slithered in. This could get dangerous. I wonder if there'll be a fight—oh wow, oh she's chucking a spready.'

'She's twerking a storm, backing into a dick, a giant pink pill, more presenting, group presenting aaaand chorus time.'

'This section is more minge-focused. Every 0.7 seconds there's a lot of minge in ya face. I have totally lost faith in this song being about a large non-venomous *Eunectes murinus* anaconda.'

'This is a song about a big dick wanting to anal-fuck a big arse but, you know, don't say it like that; it might hinder ya marketing.'

'Do I need to watch the pornification of mainstream pop music when I can just access hardcore porn and play it to me own soundtrack?'

'There's a bloke getting felt up. He doesn't quite know what to do with himself, so he intellectually strokes his chin, pondering the meaning of arse.'

'Overall, I really do just see this song being about anal fucking when you're on drugs. Whatever floats ya boat!'

OZZY MAN REFLECTS ...

Reflecting on this commentary, I'd say it's some of my most scathing work to date. Gee whizz. I was angry about life in 2014. I mean, I stand by it—'Anaconda' is a very sleazy music video—but if ya watch the whole review again . . . I was angry. Maybe I still am, and I never realise I'm angry until I reflect. This reflection segment of the book is going to be an enlightening journey of self-awareness for me, eh!

'Anaconda' is the only music video I've done a commentary on. I suck at sequels.

I haven't enjoyed mainstream pop music since I was a teenager— an angry teenager, who has morphed into an angry adult. The superficiality pisses me off. It makes me angry (again) to think that The Beatles used to be considered the definition of the pop genre, but now pop is less about talent, skill and creative exploration than it is about marketing and ramming artists down a certain demographic's throat. Fuck that! Maybe it's me, though. Maybe I'm entering the beginning of a life chapter where I don't realise that I'm old, or that I'm getting old. The phase where I yell and rant about how I 'don't get what the kids are into'.

Me favourite bands and musicians: The Beatles (clearly), AC/DC, Pearl Jam, Nick Cave, Nirvana and Hans Zimmer.

Oh, by the way . . . the green *Eunectes murinus* anaconda is also known as the common anaconda or water boa. It is a non-venomous boa species found in South America. Now you've learnt something.

Source video: NickiMinajAtVevo

Ozzy Man Reviews
WTF HAPPENED IN MARCH 2015

Released: 1 April 2015 on YouTube and Facebook

'A wild pig trespasses in a pony field and gets chased. This has been a stark reminder for the world that you should not fuck with ponies.'

'Two koalas also got in a fight this month. To be honest, it was nice to see them do something other than sleep and eat fucken eucalyptus leaves all day.'

I AM TRYING TO FIGURE OUT
HOW HUMANS HAVE MADE IT
ALL THE WAY TO 2017!

OZZY MAN REVIEWS

'Another sick moment in March was seeing Eddie Hall lift heavy shit with Arnie yelling, "Come on, do it!" "Yeah I bloody am doing it, Arnie."'

'Natalia Kills acted like a fair dinkum tosser on *The X Factor*. Apparently the dickhead on the left has copyrighted hair and suits.'

'A baby elephant realises bath time is pretty good fun.'

'Overall, it's been an epic month of lightsaber battles, hungry Brazilian piranhas, amazing squirrels ...'

'... and humans taking fucken deadly risks.'

OZZY MAN REFLECTS ...

I've always enjoyed strange news as much as legitimate world news and this monthly series is a reflection of that. As a kid, I enjoyed *The Guinness Book of Records* and the TV show *Ripley's Believe It or Not!* I try to include stories of bizarre accomplishments (or failures) mixed in with some big issues and news each month. I was very happy when this series appeared to catch on; the most dedicated subscribers to Ozzy Man are usually saying 'WTF happened last month?' within the first week of a new month to ensure I make the next episode ASAP.

This series is currently in its third year, and I put about twenty different videos and stories in each month's compilation. It's a big research, editing and writing job that often requires a mid-strength beer and a Panadol upon completion.

Some months are genuinely funnier than other months. It's bloody difficult to make this series when too much intense shit happens in a month—divisive politics, terror attacks and beloved celebrities committing suicide all have to be recapped and documented . . . But, yeah, it can be demotivating in the quiet months, and difficult to get started on an episode. I do enjoy looking out for strange, freakish and humorous stories each month, though!

Source videos, from start of section: (1) Jukin Video; (2, 3) Storyful and Ashton Webster; (4) Tim Dinte, YouTube; (5) Mediaworks and Fremantle Media; (6) Claus Jorgensen, YouTube; (7) Jukin Video; (8) bhminden, YouTube; (9) National Geographic

Ozzy Man Reviews
GAME OF THRONES
SEASON 6, EP 9
Released: 21 June 2016 on YouTube and Facebook

'Jonno is stuck in some kinda horse-pinball machine. C'mon, give him something to work with . . .'

'There it is. Fuck yes! Now he's getting some runs on the board! Look behind ya, mate! Look behind ya! Ah, no worries. Get fucked, cunt! Ouch. Nah, I dunno about this. I don't wanna play anymore.'

'I didn't think things could get worse, but now Jonno's army is fucken surrounded.'

'Crikey. Now it's become worse than being in a mosh pit at a Limp Bizkit concert.'

'And there's Littlefinger's army. Fuck, I love Littlefinger. Oi, yeah nah, I always have. Him and Sansa are the new Gandalf.'

'Wun Wun breaks through the doors of Winterfell. Unfortunately, he gets turned into a pin cushion.'

'Finally, Jonno makes it within punching distance of Ramsay and knocks his block off something chronic.'

OZZY MAN REFLECTS ...

The *Game of Thrones* recaps and reviews are where it all began for me. It was the first kind of content I made on YouTube in April 2014. Editing the visuals and writing at the same time is a slow and steady process, but I chip away at it and get there in the end! Once the timing is all worked out, I add the energy during the voice-over recording. Each *GoT* recap and review is around 1500 words in total. It's like writing a fucken essay a week during each season of the show.

I've chosen a snippet from the 'Battle of the Bastards' recap and review because it's one of my favourite episodes ever. The emotion between characters and the pacing of the action sequences all work so well together. It's fair dinkum intense as fuck. The director of that episode, Miguel Sapochnik, totally deserved the Emmy Award for Best Director. Anyhow, I'll quit kissing arse. If ya don't watch *GoT* or haven't read *A Song of Ice and Fire*, you're missing out on some extraordinary times.

Seasons 4 and 6 are my favourite *Thrones* seasons to date. I'm loyal to House Stark. Call me a sucker for punishment . . .

Source video: HBO

Ozzy Man Reviews
YANET GARCÍA & MEXICAN WEATHER

Released: 3 July 2015 on YouTube and Facebook

CONDICIONES ACTUALES

Temperatura
27°

Viento: NE 5 KMH
Humedad: 74%
Presión: 1012 Mbs.

@ IAMYANETGARCIA   26°

'I find myself really interested in Mexican weather lately. I dunno what it is—aw, fuck me.'

'I get the bullet points. I get the bloody bullet points and that's all ya need. Mínima. Máxima. Noche.'

'She'd make me approach the apocalypse with a can-do attitude.'

'If I did know Spanish and Yanet told me that a freak tidal wave was approaching, I'd be like . . . "So what? I'll live. It's no worries. I have a snorkel."'

OZZY MAN REFLECTS ...

Some days making a comedy video can fall into place effortlessly: the concept is good, the source footage is dynamic, the editing motors along, and the script and voice-over work flows like a river. This was one of those videos where all the elements converged. It's one of my funniest (based on the amount of people who quote lines from it) and it spread like wildfire on both YouTube and Facebook. Of course, the majority of the credit here goes to Yanet García. She has completely changed the modern climate of weather reporting.

My commentary has nearly 13 million views on YouTube, and at least three different companies have attempted to copyright claim and redirect all advertising monetisation to their businesses. I stand by the work as being satirical and transformative enough to be recognised as a new work. But despite efforts to explain my comedy writing, my video has been taken down and reinstated *twice* on YouTube under the Digital Millennium Copyright Act, blah blah blah.

I wanted to pitch my tone as horny, not creepy. That's an important line to draw in the sand when taking on sexual humour. Personally, I enjoy sexual humour. Despite our continual technological advancements, we're not fucken robots free of human feelings and a need to express them . . . yet. The execution is key, that's all.

I have no doubt Yanet and her boyfriend, Doug, are aware of the video. (I should say *videos*. I made a Yanet García sequel a year later. Oh fuck, I did also review her lingerie video. Okay, okay, okay, I've made three Yanet videos in total. No biggie.) Yanet does not seem fazed and Doug doesn't wanna kill me, so that's a fucken big win, I reckon!

Source video: Televisa Monterrey and iamYanetGarcia, YouTube

Ozzy Man & Mozza Commentate
A KANGAROO STREET FIGHT
Released: 27 November 2014 on YouTube and Facebook

'Welcome to fight day! We got Skippy on the right, fresh off his crushing defeat of Kangaroo Jack. His opponent today is the very dangerous Captain Kangaroo.'

'And he doesn't know that Skippy's been drinking! It's ON!'

'There's one, two, three kicks. Four, five, six. OHHH, that one landed hard!'

'He took six good, hard shots to the spoof factory in the space of ten seconds. He is done for.'

OZZY MAN REFLECTS ...

The street setting for this video made it unique, and the fight between the bloody roos was not too shabby at all. However, I clearly could not think of a satisfying way to end it, so after six beers I decided to add explosive visual effects. I suppose in a story sense there's some dystopian kangaroo fight-club rules going on, like 'if ya leave the fight ring you explode'. (I think I got this idea from a sci-fi prison movie. Inmates would try to leave and their heads would explode due to a tracking collar around their necks. I think that's a real film.)

I did not continue to add many visual effects in the video-editing process after this episode. I tried to make an action film outta this video and my VFX skills are cringe-worthy—I'm happy to give up on developing those skills. One of my all-time favourite YouTubers is Freddie Wong. I tried to be like Freddie Wong with this video. Oh fuck it, I stand by it. I'm gonna be stubborn. I like the video and my remix of it, damn it!

Mozza is a comedian from Perth, who also goes by the name Werzel on stage. He is a bloke of many identities. We first met in 2003 when I was seventeen and wanted to perform stand-up comedy at a weekly club he ran called the Comedy Lounge. It was in a bar called the Hyde Park Hotel. Eddie Vedder went to that pub once. Fuck yes. Mozza told me I was utter shit after my first gig and that I should fuck off and die . . . Not really. He's the nicest fella you'll ever meet and a stellar live performer.

Think of Mozza as the Kramer in the Ozzy Man universe. You never knew when Kramer would slide through the door into Jerry's apartment in *Seinfeld*; it's kinda the same on me YouTube channel and Facebook page. Mozza pops in whenever he feels like it. Some years more than others.

Ozzy Man Reviews
COWS VS TURTLE
Released: 1 February 2017 on YouTube and Facebook

'Here we have some cows investigating a strange, unknown object.'

'The white cow is like, "We're being invaded. There's a breach in the paddock, everyone!"'

'The grey cow whispers, "I knew this day would come. It's the fucken prophecy." Everyone says, "Shut the fuck up", but he keeps spreading doomsday propaganda.'

'"Oi, Shirley, can you move this rock?" Shirley says, "Fuck off, I'm heading to the bomb shelter."'

'In comes a baby. He's like, "It's just a rock, or a meteorite, or a piece of horseshit—OH, it fucken took a swing at me!"'

'The turtle is victorious. The cows are yelling, "Run away! Run away, everyone! Get to the fucken muster point. This is not a drill. Run away in a calm, orderly fashion please."'

OZZY MAN REFLECTS ...

Cows are one of my favourite animals to commentate over. I think it has something to do with the fact that they often appear confused about life or hesitant towards risk. I can relate to cows. Or maybe I just enjoy projecting my feelings on to them and their dopey fucken faces. Under Chinese astrology I was born in the year of the ox, so it's the cumbersome and dim-witted-looking animals in the world I connect with the most.

Another cow-based commentary video I enjoyed producing in 2017 was the one where they watch a sheila doing handstands and yoga. Seeing a human contort her body in a few different ways seemed to genuinely freak the gentle beasts out. I'm always on the hunt for more quality cow content.

Overall, you can put me down as being a fan of cows. Maybe I'll make a spin-off YouTube channel and Facebook page 100 per cent dedicated to cow content. Nothing else. Cow pictures, cow videos, cow articles, cow giveaways, cow Q&As, cow polls, cow quizzes, 24 posts a day. Yeah! Or maybe I can do Cow Week, like how the Discovery Channel does Shark Week. Who's with me?! Hmm . . . Nah, can't be fucked.

Ozzy Man Reviews
MEN'S DIVING

Released: 11 August 2015 on YouTube and Facebook

'Johnno Fabriga, bloody Fabsy, up first. He's looking graceful as he gets ready to launch into a triple backflip—oh, he's fucked it big time!'

'If this was a big splash competition, nailed it. Sincerely, fantastic splash.'

'His teammate gives him some skin. It's worth celebrating a score of zero. I mean, yeah nah, it's not about winning.'

'Pahoyo up next.'

'He starts off with his determined face, determined face, determined face, and then it's right about here he gives up and has to hope for the best.'

OZZY MAN REFLECTS ...

This video massively grew my fan base in the Philippines. Between the Ozzy Man Reviews Facebook page, the Viral Thread page and the Lad Bible page, it was viewed a fuckload of times. Funny thing is, it took about a year to catch on. I made it in 2015, but it went big in August 2016 as the Rio Olympics was on. Is this what the movie industry calls a 'sleeper hit'? Did I have a sleeper hit in regards to a web media video? I think so.

It also goes to show that older content can suddenly find a new burst of relevancy on the internet at any time. It's always a pleasant surprise when a video spikes in views and shares outta nowhere. You get to say to yourself, 'I knew it was good. I bloody knew it all along! Finally, wankers around the world appreciate it.' You then get to call it a day and hit the pub for a Coopers Sparkling Ale.

People have told me that the athletes put on a shit performance as a form of protest. If that's true, it's pretty bloody noble. I dunno how many people would inflict pain on themselves via a belly flop in the pool to show they stand by their ethics, principles and beliefs.

I made myself laugh towards the end of this video. You can hear it in the final segment when the blokes high-five each other in the spa. I think it's always a good sign if I make myself laugh first and foremost.

Source video: 28th SEA Games Singapore and Sport Singapore, YouTube

Ozzy Man Reviews
BUNNY VS DOGS
Released: 7 March 2017 on YouTube and Facebook

'Welcome to the middle of butt-fuck nowhere and there is a bunny on the run from two dodgy dogs. The bunny gets cocky. He's yelling out, "Come at me, ya dim-witted mutts. Humans use me as a mascot for their fucken batteries. I can run all day. I can root all day. You got nothing on me, ya dopey fuckwits."'

'The bunny is saying, "I am everywhere. I am nowhere. I'm Keyser Söze. I'm Tyler fucken Durden. You can't see me."'

INSTANT REPLAY

'The dogs reply, "Cash me ousside. How bow dah?" The bunny says, "Gee, that's original. Do you get all your comebacks from dank memes?"'

'There's more action than a Michael Bay movie here.'

'And the bunny has vanished! Fuck yes, bunny. Fuck yes, mate.'

OZZY MAN REFLECTS ...

This is such a mysterious video, this one! It was sent to me multiple times, but finding information on where and when it was shot is tricky as fuck. The quality is horrendous, but I'm dead serious when I say there's more action than a Michael Bay movie in this video. It's edge-of-ya-seat, adrenaline-fuelled, high-octane insanity. Thinking back to the days when I was a kid and watched David Attenborough docos, the most thrilling ones were always the fucken chase scenes. This is a classic chase video overall.

The 'cash me ousside' girl was becoming a living meme in the week I made this video. I like to figure out ways I can get in on a trend without directly making content around the trend. Doing that through wildlife dialogue and banter is ideal.

I'm ecstatic the bunny got away! It was not his time. It was not the bunny's time. Gotta love a video with a happy ending in this cold, harsh, mad world.

Source video: Run Rabbit Run, Liveleak (original videographer unknown)

Ozzy Man Reviews
STEREOSONIC
Released: 2 December 2015 on YouTube and Facebook

'Stereosonic 2015, ladies and gents.'

'Because of drugs most people do end up forgetting where they are and who they are.'

'This fella thinks his body is an astral vessel connected to no one and everyone, including all animals, all trees and toasters.'

'If you start feeling queasy make sure you have a puke. Feel free to puke any time, anywhere, and on anyone.'

'I'm pretty sure this bloke has pissed in his pants. There's a definite wet patch.'

'If at any time you fall on ya head during the event, it doesn't really matter because ya head only contains ya brain.'

OZZY MAN REFLECTS ...

DJs with decent Facebook pages got hold of this video and reposted it, which ended up making it go viral. (I hate the word 'viral', by the way. Sorry I said it. It's not my intent to infect people or have my videos aligned with the spread of diseases 'n' shit.) Anyway, I don't mind reposts, as it all ends up being promotion I never would've had otherwise. There's only so much I'll police people when I myself am pushing fair-dealing laws to the absolute max.

Here's a behind-the-scenes story for ya: I was contacted by someone who said they were friends with one of the festival-goers in the video. I was told that the person had committed suicide and the spread of my video was responsible. My conscience went into hyper drive. I spent a couple of days tracking down the alleged dead dancer and messaging his social-media accounts. He was alive. He replied. He said he loved the video and the commentary was fine—and funny. I guess I was pranked for whatever reason. Anyhow, I sighed with relief and headed to the pub.

Despite the suicide being utter bullshit, it made me think about my 'social responsibility'. It was at this point that my YouTube channel and Facebook page were getting bigger and I needed to start putting real thought into who and what I would cover and the impact it could have. These days people will generally know they've appeared in an Ozzy Man video within a few hours of it being posted. It doesn't matter where they are in the world—the 'six degrees of separation' thing is real. With this in mind, I've made an internal policy to only use mean names like dickhead, cockhead, wanker, fuckhead, fuckwit, fuck-knuckle, cunt, pussy or arsehole for wildlife. Or *Game of Thrones* characters (not the actors). Real-life people doing odd things will endure some scathing sarcasm, but very rarely do I dish out any name-calling.

Source video: Stereosonic Exposed, Facebook

Ozzy Man Reviews
DUCK VS TIGER

Released: 14 February 2017 on YouTube and Facebook

'Welcome to fight day. It's duck vs tiger.'

'The tiger is looking to end this fast, but the duck fucken vanishes! He's like a little Houdini.'

'The duck says, "I reckon you should've been born a snail. HAHAHA!" The tiger has no comeback for that. I can't believe it's the duck that's doing all the roasting.'

'Down goes the duck again. He's swimming under the water aaand he rises. "Quack quack, motherfucker. Even a sloth is faster than you."'

'The tiger is getting fed up with all the insults so he lashes out!'

'In the end, the tiger says, "Screw this, I'm just gonna tell everyone I caught the duck and killed it anyway." The duck says, "That would be the dissemination of fake news, ya dodgy cunt. No one in the zoo is gonna believe ya."'

OZZY MAN REFLECTS ...

This is one of those videos which is funny in its raw form. You can watch a duck run circles around a tiger without commentary and it'll cheer you up. It'll get ya day off to a fun start. However, the main opportunity I could see in this video was to vocally turn the duck into a smart-arse with the devil-may-care attitude turned up to eleven.

The writing challenge I set for myself here was to see how many times the duck could insult the tiger. I grabbed every chance to turn him into a complete chatterbox. I love animal videos where there's potential for dialogue. They don't always have to be action-packed. As long as there's a few beats of action and some golden dialogue opportunities, then I'm happy as fuck.

I think the line 'Quack quack, motherfucker' subconsciously came from watching Samuel L. Jackson movies over and over as a teenager. It sounds more like Samuel L. Jackson than Ozzy Man. Bugger it, North American cinema and pop culture runs deep in Ozzy Man. That's probably not unnatural for an Aussie, when ya think about it. We watch more American-produced shit down here than we do Australian-produced shit.

The original video was shot at the Symbio Wildlife Park in New South Wales. The quality of the videos they're shooting over there is next-level shit. It seems like a great park, and I'll definitely have to visit 'em soon!

Source video: Symbio Wildlife Park NSW

Ozzy Man Reviews
AFL VS SOCCER BIG HIT

Released: 17 April 2016 on YouTube and Facebook

'Martin taps it along, Ablett tickles him. Aw, fuck me dead! His face, neck and spinal cord are gonna be munted from that hit.'

THE GABBA, BRISBANE

MAY MADNESS OVERSHADOWS Q-CLASH EPIC

'Look at the cagey bloody veteran. Ablett says, "Off ya go. There's the landing strip." BANG! Destination fucked.'

THE GABBA, BRISBANE

MAY MADNESS OVERSHADOWS Q-CLASH EPIC

'Meanwhile, over at the soccer. Another bloody brutal hit! Look at that!'

OZZY MAN REFLECTS ...

This video is close to my heart. I've been a Brisbane Lions supporter since 1994, when they were the Bears. Stefan Martin got absolutely shit-mixed here. I don't genuinely think Gazza Ablett was being too dodgy (maybe a little), but I wasn't gonna let an opportunity to take the piss out of a superstar slip by me.

I've made a few more videos where I cross over to the soccer to see how many players are taking a dive and faking injuries. I think I've become a troll towards soccer and fans of the sport. (If you're angry with these commentaries, it means my dodgy trolling has succeeded. Stay calm, soccer fans. Stay calm. If you're yelling 'It's called FOOTBALL!' right now . . . it also means I win. Take a breath, mate.) Okay, okay, I don't 100 per cent hate the sport, but gee whizz it is fun as fuck to satirise alongside other contact sports.

This is the video in which the catchphrase 'Destination fucked' was coined. It's a catchphrase I've learnt is relevant for many scenarios in life. I love that people can apply it to their own lives and any bullshit they may be going through. It's truly taken on a life of its own, that catchphrase.

Source video: Australian Football League and Danish Football Association

Ozzy Man Reviews
AN OCTOPUS EATING A CRAB
Released: 22 February 2015 on YouTube and Facebook

'Welcome to the outback. We're in the south of Western Australia and there's a crab!'

'It does a cheeky crab walk down to the pond to look for some tucker.'

'Things that can fuck ya up in Australia are snakes, crocodiles, John Jarratt, spiders, immigration officers—HAWW! Fuck me dead, it's an octopus! What a spectacular tackle!'

'The slimy wanker creeps back into its dark evil lair to digest the crab and grow to a freakish size.'

OZZY MAN REFLECTS ...

The raw video of this one is as perfect as it gets. It's a video where someone was in the right place at the right time. It's the perfect video for Ozzy Man to lose his shit over. I mean, where the fuck did that octopus come from all of a sudden?! Filming a massive crab was exciting enough—I'd consider a commentary on a massive crab doing bugger all—but the fact it turned into an MMA Fight Night outta nowhere was pure gold. I hope this video and my commentary of it ages well online.

This showdown took place in Yallingup, Western Australia—the same town where Pearl Jam wrote the song 'Elderly Woman Behind the Counter in a Small Town'. Between PJ visiting in the nineties and this epic wildlife fight, I'd say Yallingup should remain famous for ages, eh. I sound like I stalk Eddie Vedder every time he comes to Perth.

The line about immigration officers being able to fuck you up was improvised during the voice-over. My missus was applying for her next visa to stay in Australia. Although we mostly spoke to good-natured government officers over the phone during this era (that's not sarcasm—I actually think lots of officers down under do a great job), our frustration at the level of work we were required to do needed to be cheekily vented somewhere. See what I did there? Bloody see what I did? Whacked a dollop of real-life experience into the online comedy. It's not the first time, nor the last.

Source video: ViralHog

Ozzy Man Reviews
FUNNIEST KICKBOXING MATCH EVER

Released: 18 February 2016 on YouTube and Facebook

'Get a look at these silky skills.'

'The ref is like, "What are ya doing? You getting up? You staying down? You going home?" Red pants guy is like, "Nah, I'm fucken good. Let's fight."'

'Blue pants fella is getting a lot of punches in.'

'Fucken SONIC BOOM. Take that.'

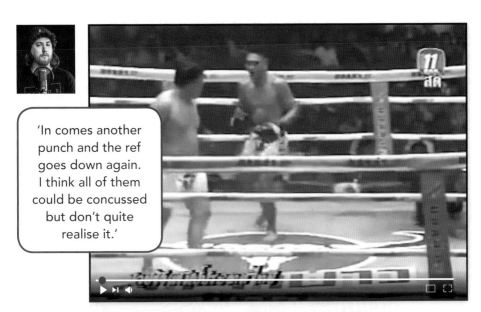

'In comes another punch and the ref goes down again. I think all of them could be concussed but don't quite realise it.'

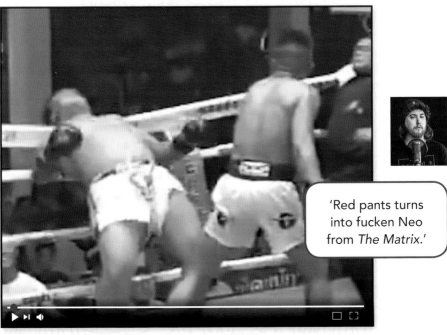

'Red pants turns into fucken Neo from *The Matrix*.'

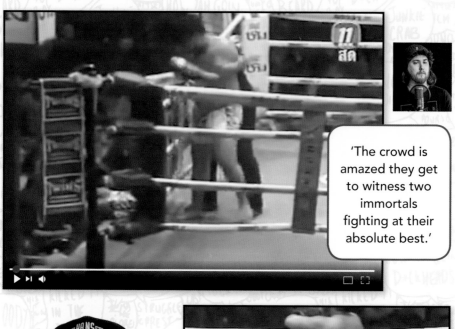

'The crowd is amazed they get to witness two immortals fighting at their absolute best.'

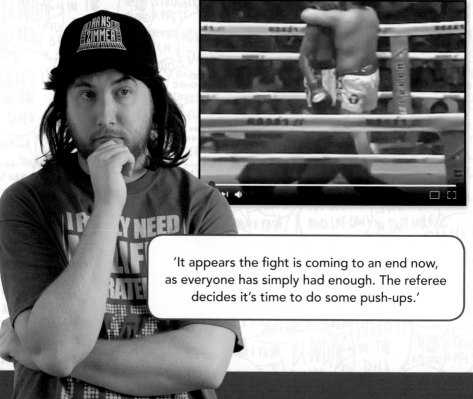

'It appears the fight is coming to an end now, as everyone has simply had enough. The referee decides it's time to do some push-ups.'

OZZY MAN REFLECTS ...

Fuck yes, Thailand. Fuck yes. Enough said.

Source video: Broadcasting Services of Thailand, Chong sib-ed (Channel 11)

Ozzy Man Reviews
GRANDPA VS BROWN SNAKE

Released: 30 November 2015 on Facebook

'I dunno how well ya can see it but next to the grass over there is a brown snake, one of Australia's most venomous.'

'Oh no, it's an innocent geriatric. Look out, dickhead, veer left.'

'The old-timer kicks it in its fucken face!'

'Nothing is coming between this bloke and his 10 a.m. mid-strength beer at the bowls club.'

OZZY MAN REFLECTS ...

Due to some licensing debacles at the time, I only made this one available on Facebook (not YouTube and Facebook). I might look to get it up on the YouTube channel soon, because people do cite it as one of their favourites quite a lot. It feels like it did well in my home country of Australia! I think we like the idea of a tough old digger, an Aussie battler, giving zero fucks about taking on a brown snake. It's fair dinkum brilliant source material to work with.

I think the fella's identity is still unknown. The location of this epic battle has been recognised as the Nobby's Beach Surf Life Saving Club in Queensland. Fuck yes, Nobby's Beach. Fuck yes!

Eastern brown snakes can be aggressive little wankers and are responsible for 60 per cent of snake-bite deaths down under (that's what Wikipedia reckons). I'm lucky enough to have never encountered one. I came close to a death adder once. Those snakes are badass as well.

Source video: Jukin Video

Ozzy Man Reviews
INDECISIVE LIONESS HUNTING

Released: 19 December 2015 on YouTube and Facebook

'Have a look at this lioness. She's out doing the grocery shopping and cannot make a fucken decision on which brand of meat to choose.'

'Look at her judging them. I don't want that one; it's got a skinny arse. That one has no thighs. That wanker has a stupid look on his face. That one has a child; I can't kill her.'

'Aw but look at this! In comes hubby and says, "Just fucken pick something! We don't need a fucken salad either!"'

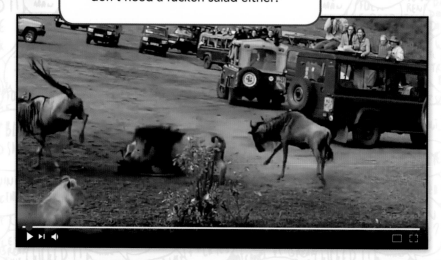

OZZY MAN REFLECTS ...

This video spread like wildfire across multiple pages on Facebook. I chose the source video because I loved the twist at the end, where the bloke lion comes sprinting in and takes down the wildebeest. It's rare for a source video to have such a great natural ending. Usually I have to work towards a twist with some creative editing, or a decent line of dialogue that results in a punchline at the very least. There's a sizeable trove of tourist videos shot in Africa on the web and a lot of footage that's just gold. Videos shot in Kruger National Park in particular seem to get fairly chaotic.

The line 'Just fucken pick something!' when the lion eventually runs in appeared to resonate with many people. I witnessed a lot of men and women tagging each other.

I've always enjoyed relationship comedy. Not so much the jaded and bitter tone of relationship comedy, but the playful tone (think Jerry Seinfeld and Chris Rock). This video was a turning point for me and I started looking for ways to put human emotions and behaviour into animal commentaries. I find that when I put relatable human stuff into the animal commentaries it can be fucken funny.

Source video: Jukin Video

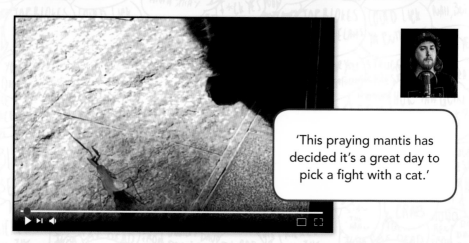

'This praying mantis has decided it's a great day to pick a fight with a cat.'

'The cat says, "What are you actually trying to achieve?"'

'Mantis gets dragged across the ground! He keeps being cheeky and calls the cat a fuckhead, so he gets dragged across the ground again. The cat turns to the human: "Are you filming this? Can you believe this guy? He's insane."'

'The cat says, "Stop doing that silly pose."'

'He swipes and the mantis has got him! It's turned into a fucken rodeo!'

'Cat says, "Look, you're really rude and annoying and the fake eyes you painted on your wings look terrible, but I'm looking for a new crime-fighting partner and you've got what it takes, so maybe we could be a team?"'

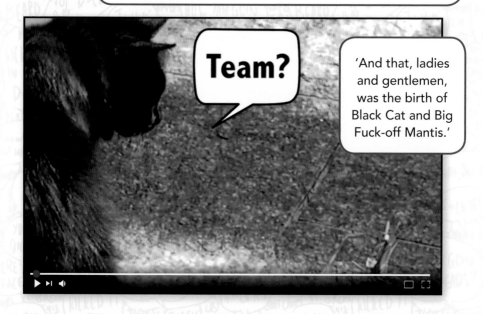

Team?

'And that, ladies and gentlemen, was the birth of Black Cat and Big Fuck-off Mantis.'

OZZY MAN REFLECTS ...

This is one of my personal favourites when it comes to my wildlife commentaries. It's such a unique showdown. It was a great source video to work with because it's absolutely an unfair fight. The mantis could've surely been squashed to death if the cat had landed one clean hit. I'd say it's a great video because the mantis is the underdog and manages to turn the tables. It's a classic underdog story. It's the web-video version of *Rocky*!

You gotta wonder why humans never stop their pet from fighting another creature right in front of 'em. I guess we have a morbid curiosity for seeing how things will turn out without our bloody intervention all the time, eh? Thankfully, the mantis appeared to get out of this battle unscathed, and in my simple little mind I thoroughly enjoy the narrative that they've started a superhero squad.

There's potential for a comic-book spin-off from this video, I reckon.

Ozzy Man Reviews
RIO OLYMPICS HIGHLIGHTS #1

Released: 10 August 2016 on YouTube and Facebook

'There's been plenty of backflips, twists and AWW—a self-inflicted pile driver.'

'Look away now, look away now, look away now. I've warned you. Aw, the Frenchman. Fuck, he's boarding a flight to destination fucked.'

'Sun Yang does a ninja jump and his cap lands on the head of a jovial old fella.'

'Yep, that is the look of a man who knows he's swallowed a fuck ton of dodgy water.'

'Butt and Fuchs have finally come together. They are a great combo.'

OZZY MAN REFLECTS ...

I only did two Rio Olympics commentaries because the copyright policing around the footage was next-level shit. The International Olympic Committee (IOC) was sending out takedowns on everything uploaded to do with the games. It was a real shame that the IOC didn't wish to allow sporting-fan communities to flourish online; I suppose their deals with traditional broadcasters meant all footage had to be centralised to one distribution channel. Anyhow, I stand by my commentary as being a transformative work and I reckon it's unlikely to cause fucken market harm to the main broadcast. I took the piss out of the games while still being sincerely enthusiastic about 'em. I have genuinely loved the Olympics since I was a kid.

Anyway, every week is like walking through a copyright and censorship minefield for me. I never know how media companies will react to having a vulgar Australian yelling over their footage. Seeking permission to remix and mash up big media footage is usually a dead end, so I simply have to go for it and gauge what the reaction is from a company afterwards. It's not an ideal way to work at all, but it always keeps things fresh. The creativity is prioritised over legalities. You may say I'm not the sharpest tool in the shed for operating that way. That's fine. Thankfully, the Rio commentaries were reinstated on YouTube after the games came to an end.

Bring on Tokyo 2020!

Source video: International Olympic Committee

Ozzy Man & Mozza Commentate
BUNNY VS SNAKE
Released: 17 August 2015 on YouTube and Facebook

'Welcome back, everyone, to another fight day.'

'What we're witnessing is a home invasion, Ozzy. A snake appears to have broken into a bunny nest and is strangling the kids.'

'It's not pretty.'

'Nah it's fucked.'

'AWWWWW! Big mama is in the house!'

'I thought I was commentating a quiet lunch, but this is a FAIR DINKUM SHITFIGHT.'

'She bites down on the snake, 1000 kicks, 2000 kicks, 3000 kicks—'

'4000-kick combo!'

'The snake is off now. The rabbit says, "Oh cheers. Thanks. Don't forget ya gift bag, cunt!"'

OZZY MAN REFLECTS ...

In its raw form, this video was quite long and absolute chaos in terms of the action, so it made the editing difficult. From memory, it took about five re-edits to nail the transitions between all the frenetic moments and the slower moments. When I say five re-edits, it was probably more like twenty. I'm a meticulous video editor. The scripting and the video editing go hand in hand. I will tinker with a video and my writing until it can be tinkered with no more. There's always a way to tighten a story further (even if it's just a crass and vulgar online commentary) to make sure it's all killer and no filler!

It's a rough video to watch when ya think about it. It looks like only one baby bunny survived! I don't often tackle videos with death in them (animal or human), but there was no intervention here from people so that made it easier to approach ethically. It all appears to go down naturally in the raw video. Nature is a brutal thing, but we can get levity and LOLs out of its bloody brutality.

Moz was truly emotional on this day. This video was an outlet for him, I believe. The line 'Don't forget ya gift bag, cunt!' was not in our original script. That was raw emotion and improvised. It's my favourite line from the video.

Source video: Momma Rabbit, YouTube

Ozzy Man Reviews
CLOWNS

Released: 10 October 2016 on YouTube and Facebook

'We have currently been witnessing one of the greatest clown epidemics of our time.'

'How harmful can this guy be? It's daytime. Aw, he's got a machete! Okay. Maybe these wankers are going a little too far. Yep, time to shit yourself and run away.'

'Here's one for the kids. "Come look at the security footage. It's Halloween time. Don't be scared. That's Uncle Terry. It's ya dad's brother. He's jobless."'

'This guy wants to let his dog on ya, and the dog's not in the mood for any fucken clowning around. And there it is, the punchline: a panicked, crying teenage boy.'

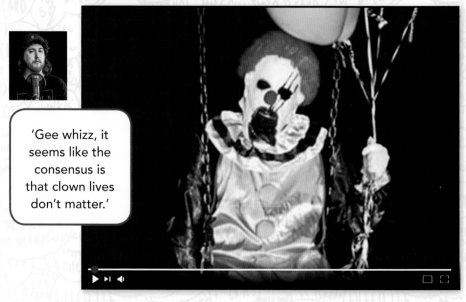

'Gee whizz, it seems like the consensus is that clown lives don't matter.'

OZZY MAN REFLECTS ...

You may've noticed there's a recurring character in my commentary videos called Uncle Terry. He is entirely fictional. I don't have an Uncle Terry, unfortunately. Any likeness to a real uncle of mine by a different name is purely coincidental—just to make sure we've cleared that potential legality issue up.

I dunno what it's usually like in North America during Halloween, but it definitely seemed like the clown intensity was high in 2016. It looked like there was a greater number of freaky bastards than usual going around. It's good to have a hobby, I guess, even if it results in people wanting to beat the shit out of ya.

I reckon it was mostly my American audience that got a chuckle from this one. Maybe the United Kingdom, too. They definitely give more fucks about Halloween than Australia does. The majority of Australians give zero fucks about Halloween. I do enjoy being in America during Halloween, though. It's impressive. I went to a Halloween Horror Night at Universal Studios in Los Angeles circa 2009. I wasn't scared. I'm not a chicken. (I may've been a tad scared.) I don't believe in ghosts. I love supernatural stories, but I don't believe 'em for a second. I don't believe in much. I don't leave the house much. I don't do much overall. I'm still fun at a party, however.

Source videos, from start of section: (1) CBS Chicago and Brad Graham, YouTube; (2) Leaferbag, YouTube; (3) News4Jax; (4) HelloGum, YouTube; (5) Rangel Photography (SSR)

Ozzy Man Reviews
PEOPLE FUCKED UP BY BULLS

Released: 4 April 2016 on YouTube and Facebook

'Aw, she takes one right up the butthole.'

'You big bloody dickhead, you're a fucken play toy. Massive hang time!'

'Surely the bull can't jump—aw, yes it can! Huge head-butt. I don't think this bloke has a lot of brains so it's no worries. You can fucken tell this bloke is an Aussie or British tourist, can't ya.'

'This guy is wearing his Fast Pants . . . but, I tell ya what, they're ruined. His Fast Pants have been butchered, and probably his stomach too.'

'What can the ponytail fella do? Sweet fuck all. He's literally gonna lie down and wait for all of this to blow over.'

'The bull appears to be starting some form of new transportation business.'

'You're moving too slow—aw, he's exploded! He took a horn in the pooffoo valve and turned to red mist. Wait a second, there's a head . . . nah, he's all right.'

OZZY MAN REFLECTS ...

I've never paid much attention to the Running of the Bulls in Spain. I'm not supportive, but nor am I hypercritical of the tradition. I guess in general I'm curious . . . I'm curious because there's no way in hell you're ever gonna get me to have a go at this, so it makes me ponder why others enjoy it.

I discovered that bull-related content is a very heated topic online. It's not as heated as discussing vaccination or feminism or Donald Trump, but nonetheless it's bloody heated. I don't mind doing commentary over intense footage where people end up with serious injuries, but the social networks don't like it so much these days, as they have to be 'advertiser friendly'. So, any footage where injuries are too graphic can mean a whole video commentary will be age-restricted, demonetised or taken down. If Donald Trump threatens nuclear war on Facebook and Twitter it's no worries, but if I take the piss out of fellas with questionable levels of intelligence getting stampeded it's deemed unsafe for the world.

The context matters when it comes to commentating violent or graphic footage. If I think solid satire and a good conversation can come out of it, then I reckon that's not bad!

I snatched the term 'pooffoo valve' from Carl Barron. It's a very niche term for your butthole. It's playful. I like it. I want to hear it used in the world more.

I've been meaning to make a sequel to this video for over a year. I'll quit being a bludger and get around to it one day.

Source video: Gabriel Alves Vieira (fotogabriel), YouTube

Ozzy Man Reviews
IGUANA VS SNAKES (BBC'S *PLANET EARTH II*)

Released: 8 November 2016 on YouTube and Facebook

'There's a young iguana walking to school by himself, and there's a pack of snakes!'

'He's like, "No worries, I can't go left. Above me is no good. Going right is fucked . . ."'

'"Oh, it fucken touched me!"'

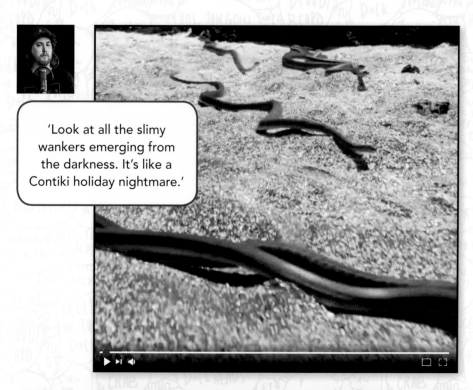

'Look at all the slimy wankers emerging from the darkness. It's like a Contiki holiday nightmare.'

'He burns around the corner, but look out! There's an ambush! Oh, fuck off.'

'No! Corrupt politicians, war in the Middle East, shorter seasons of *Game of Thrones* and now this.'

'Aw, it's all good!'

'He's like, "From this point, I just need to listen to Bear Grylls. I have to get to higher ground, start a campfire, and I'll drink my own piss."'

'Back to the darkness, ya dickhead.'

OZZY MAN REFLECTS ...

I was super-duper excited about *Planet Earth II*. I had already done a commentary on the trailer a month or two ahead of the 'Iguana vs Snakes' video. BBC Radio 1 contacted me and asked if I could make a censored version of the trailer commentary for 'em. I won't lie, it is tough when someone asks me not to fucken swear, but I thought, 'Fuck it, I'm up for the fucken challenge. Fucken bring it on, BBC.'

The non-swearing version actually came up a treat and was posted on the BBC Radio 1 Facebook page.

The 'Iguana vs Snakes' scene is from the episode 'Islands'. As soon as it aired in the UK, the scene was ripped and uploaded to a bunch of Facebook pages. It spread like crazy across the world. People were sending me links to this scene every minute for about ten hours straight. I'm not exaggerating. It was in the Ozzy Man Reviews Facebook inbox every single fucken minute. There was NO WAY I could ignore it. There was no time to consider if the BBC would allow transformative works made from the footage to remain online. I couldn't think about a copyright takedown. People wanted me to commentate it, and I have to listen my audience! I'm a slave to my audience (in a good way. Or a destructive way. Probably both ways).

Thankfully, the BBC did not issue any copyright takedowns on my commentary. They wouldn't allow it to be monetised on YouTube, but I actually liked that; it felt like a good middle ground. They don't make money off my voice, and I don't make money off their vision. My video could stay up, and that's a win!

Source video: BBC Earth

Ozzy Man Reviews
BEER DEATHS
Released: 31 March 2017 on YouTube and Facebook

'The human race has been to the moon; we invented medicine and Tim Tams. This fella wants to leave his mark too, but he's fucked it! Totally fucked it.'

'Trying to use the ATM after a few drinks is difficult. He's in struggle forest. He's murdered the beer and it explodes all over his face.'

'Here's a delivery man. First day on the job, he's excited. And now it's gonna turn into his last day on the job.'

'This bloke is excited to go on a boat, but it will have to be without a beer!' *Hello, darkness, my old friend . . .*

'This forklift driver has decided to start a war on beer. The Russians, the Chinese, the US . . . I reckon they're all gonna get involved in this one. It's absolutely fucked.'

OZZY MAN REFLECTS ...

Being a lover of beer, this is a commentary video that's very close to my heart. I take the piss outta these incidents, but in all sincerity the loss of a fresh drink is no laughing matter. I acknowledge the devastating impact it can have on ya mentally. You're thirsty, you've bought a drink, you're anticipating your first refreshing mouthful and then BAM! A freakish accident or human error sends your brew to destination fucked. We need to raise more awareness of this important issue.

I didn't realise the title of the video could be misinterpreted. Due to the name 'Beer Deaths' some folks expected this to be about people who have died because of beer. I'm all for dark comedy—big fan of dark comedy—but, yeah nah, to go that morbid was not the idea. It's about the life of beer as its own entity. Glad I cleared that up here.

My favourite beer is Coopers, made in Adelaide, South Australia. It's a fair dinkum reliable lover.

Source videos, from start of section: (1) hutzelbrot8888, YouTube; (2) Dude Stuff, YouTube; (3) Mirko Blanks, YouTube; (4) HD Broadcaster (Paul Szott), YouTube; (5) Phinel Sul de Minas

Ozzy Man Reviews
MICK FANNING VS SHARK
Released: 20 July 2015 on YouTube and Facebook

'Mick Fanning up next—fin, fin, fin! Fucken leg it, get out of there, Mick!'

'This better not be a dolphin trying to be funny.'

'Yeah nah, he's all good. I hope there's a beer in the back of that jet-ski seat—a bloody cold one on ice.'

'Here's an interview. For international viewers, I'll translate: "I was out on me bloody board, ready to win the competition. I dunno if it was a sabotage by another competitor or the shark acted alone, but all of a sudden it fucken came up and I went BLAH! I said, 'You are cruising for a bruising', and then I gave it a knuckle sandwich."'*

*May or may not be an exact translation of what Mick Fanning said.

OZZY MAN REFLECTS ...

Mick Fanning 100 per cent confirms he punched the shark in all the interviews he's done about this. That's fair dinkum hilarious! Or at least at first it seems hilarious . . . then ya put yourself in his shoes and you realise it's probably a natural reaction. Bloody fight or flight mode, eh. It's science, mate.

Having a fist fight with a shark is enough to make the Australian Hall of Fame, I reckon. The raw footage of this was massively popular and I think many Australians would agree that Mick is an Aussie hero. We don't take heroes that seriously in Australia. We're not a big hero country. We mostly use the word 'hero' in a loose and comedic way, juxtaposed with mundane achievements, or to take the piss out of someone when they make a dick outta themselves—'Ha! Ya tried to be a hero!' Mick is nonetheless an Aussie hero in a non-piss-taking way. (Okay, maybe I'm taking the piss a little. I can't tell anymore.)

I have always loved surfing and I did wanna get into it for a while. I guess I'm a big pussy. I simply love watching it. I mostly love big wave surfing, where crazy bastards get towed in with a fucken jet ski. That is next-level shit.

Source video: World Surf League

Ozzy Man Reviews
IRISH BOUNCER VS DRUNKARDS

Released: 21 November 2016 on YouTube and Facebook

'There's a sausage fest clogging up the door and it's turned into a fight!'

'The bouncer stays steady. The lanky guy charges, he throws a weak-ass punch and now the bouncer takes them down. Holy shitballs!'

'This bouncer is as reliable as The Beatles when it comes to delivering hits.'

'He's having a nap in destination fucked.'

'His mate spits on the bouncer— probably not gonna solve anything.'

'Take him home, give him a pillow, a mid-strength beer and a Panadol.'

OZZY MAN REFLECTS ...

I try to choose real-life fight videos wisely. I don't like to be sent too many of them. I like them to have an ending where you can see that everyone is relatively okay (and mainly just egos, dignity and pride are hurt).

I've never been in a drunken fight. Of course, I'm not a perfect man when I'm on the piss and full as a doctor's wallet, but I've never committed to fighting someone when I'm drunk (or sober. I think I punched a kid when I was ten—that's about it. Felt bad about it afterwards). Who knows what's going on in someone's life when they're legless from booze and wanna start shit? Ultimately, I won't judge 'em too harshly. Happy to poke fun at the whole primitive nature of hitting each other with our hands, though.

I learned from the comments section that bouncers prefer to be called 'doormen'. I like it when people with genuine personal experience and expertise join the comments section, like this:

'Sadly, I've been in the doorman's position. I dislike the term "bouncer", because it gives a negative connotation about our job duties. The majority of us in the trade are pretty laid-back guys who have a little extra size and above-average skills in self-defence, exhibiting an ability to work in high-stress situations that many folks couldn't handle. I've never really figured out why some people have an obsession with fighting us, but it's never a good idea since, as I stated before, we tend to operate on a higher level than them. This doorman did everything right. Defended himself, not going out of his way to hurt the attackers, all the while radioing for back up. Kudos. Stay safe out there.'

Source video: ViralHog

Ozzy Man Reviews
GREATEST OLYMPIC WIN EVER

Released: 15 August 2016 on YouTube and Facebook

'I'm gonna take you back to 2002 for one of the greatest moments probably in the history of the world.'

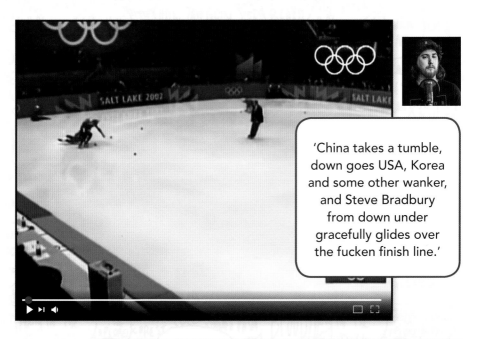

'China takes a tumble, down goes USA, Korea and some other wanker, and Steve Bradbury from down under gracefully glides over the fucken finish line.'

'Sure, some people say he was losing, but those people would be dickheads.'

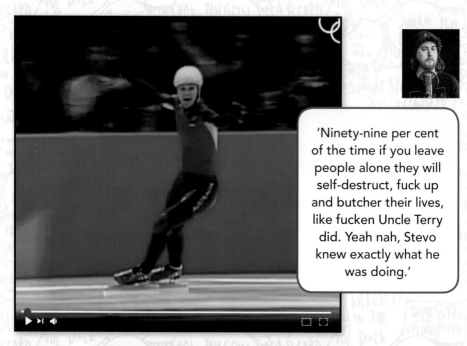

'Ninety-nine per cent of the time if you leave people alone they will self-destruct, fuck up and butcher their lives, like fucken Uncle Terry did. Yeah nah, Stevo knew exactly what he was doing.'

'Undeniable fair dinkum genius.'

OZZY MAN REFLECTS ...

The phrase 'chucking a Bradbury' or 'pulled a Bradbury' or 'doing a Bradbury' has become popular in Australia since 2002. You can use it any time you unexpectedly win at something. Whether you plotted to be a victorious underdog or it genuinely surprised you when you won, it's no worries; you can say, 'Yeah nah yeah, I just chucked a Bradbury. I am taking home the gold and no one can argue.'

Claiming this moment to be the greatest Olympic win ever is wonderfully arrogant. Just when ya think Aussies can be humble, I go ahead and bloody claim this as the greatest gold-medal moment in the history of the entire Olympics, reminding you that we're also cocky loudmouths when we wanna be down here. Yeah nah yeah, winter Olympics or summer Olympics, zero fucks given. I'm not differentiating 'em. I'm claiming this as the greatest win and no one can stop me. I assume some people disliked the video because they disliked my pretentious title. This makes the whole commentary even funnier in my book (and you're in my book right now—OHHHH! High-five, mate).

From one cheeky bastard to another, I do hope Steve Bradbury has seen my commentary on his classic win. We must make sure the world never forgets it, Stevo.

Ozzy Man Reviews
MMA 9-SECOND KNOCKOUT

Released: 7 December 2015 on YouTube and Facebook

'We got Jason Solomon here, letting the crowd know how much he loves them and touching some woman's womb. He also touches the other one's womb.'

'He gets his entourage together for a pre-match pose.'

JASON R SOLOMON

'He's gotta fucken dance a little bit before fighting.'

'Now it's hug time.'

'He finally heads into the ring and has to do a fucken trick. Ya can't enter without doing a mint trick.'

'He taunts his opponent, who is actually focused.'

'They touch gloves. He's a bit too touchy. That's okay—at least he's not chuckin' a Ronda, disregarding the ritual.'

'It's fight time, ladies and gents. He's fucken knocked out in nine seconds!'

OZZY MAN REFLECTS ...

This fight was part of Super Fight League in India. When I visited New Delhi in August 2016, I did a call-out to fans to see who wanted to come have a beer at the hotel bar with me. A friend of Jason Solomon's showed up and I thought he was there to beat the shit out of me. I was bracing myself to be knocked out. I've been knocked out once in my life. It's not a lot of fun. But it turned out he was a top bloke! He told me that Jason had watched the commentary and was rolling with the punches (haha! Pun!) of internet fame from his nine-second knockout. The raw video is as popular as my re-edited version, so he had plenty of fame to roll with.

In hindsight, I wonder if I was too harsh on Mr Solomon. I do truly respect MMA fighters, boxers and martial artists. I did tae kwon do when I was ten years old and could only get to yellow belt—the one after white (beginner) belt. It was fucken hard. The idea of fighting other people for real is nerve-wracking as hell, so yeah nah yeah nah nah nah yeah, I'm cheeky towards fighters, but I admittedly could never do what they do. Respect, mate.

Source video: Super Fight League, India

Ozzy Man Reviews
CROW VS CAT VS CAT

Released: 25 September 2016 on YouTube and Facebook

'Have a look at this cheeky crow. He flies over to the ginger cat and says, "Oi, have you seen that cat over there? Nah nah nah, I'm trying to help ya. There's a cat down there talkin' shit about ya."'

'He's gone to the other cat to say, "Oi, ya see the ginger up there? Nah nah nah, I'm on your side. He's been telling everyone that you're a big fucken pussy."'

'And it is GAME ON, ladies and gents! The crow's master plan to start a race war has worked.'

'Crow has started a fight that cannot be stopped and he knows it. Yeah, he knows it.'

OZZY MAN REFLECTS ...

I like it when I can push the writing of a silly two-minute online comedy video to have a core theme. I'm really happy with the writing for this video. It's essentially about powerful people we never hear of ('behind-the-curtain men') pulling strings to start war and conflict in the world. Yep, you heard me. The crow (okay, okay, magpie. No, crow. Magpie. Could be a crow, though?) represents a hidden power structure funding the conflict between the cats, who are unfortunately too fucken easy to manipulate. That was my intent anyhow. The majority of the time I'll work on instinct and try to discover a story as I edit footage, but sometimes I will approach a video wanting to tell a particular story under the surface; wanting to get something off my mind.

Putting aside the attempt to be an artsy wanker by working themes into my writing, it's a reasonably funny commentary video, eh.

Source video: will20091995, YouTube

Ozzy Man Reviews
CRICKET NUT SHOTS
Released: 9 January 2017 on YouTube

'Three . . . two . . . one . . . Right in the balls!'

'This sheila is like, "OMG, that was so funny", and then she makes a cock of herself. The Dick Gods are dishing out instant karma.'

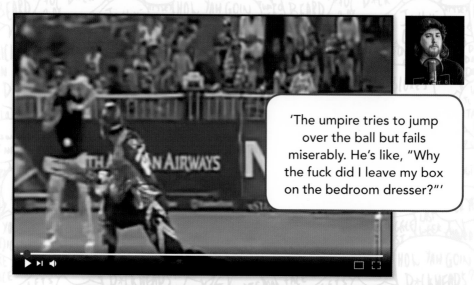

'The umpire tries to jump over the ball but fails miserably. He's like, "Why the fuck did I leave my box on the bedroom dresser?"'

'Even the great Brian Lara took one in the family jewels from time to time.'

OZZY MAN REFLECTS ...

This one's only available on my YouTube channel, but I reckon some more cricket commentaries could be a lot of fun. Billy Birmingham's audio-based cricket parody series The Twelfth Man (especially his album *Wired World of Sports*) continues to inspire my sports-based commentaries big time. His impressions of sports commentators are fair dinkum Australian comedy gold.

I do hope the majority of these players were wearing a box. The damage to the dicks in this video should not be long-term. Except for the clip of the umpire—he may not have had a box in his pants. He genuinely looked pale as fuck after that nut shot, like he was about to vomit his KFC dinner all over the field . . . Brings a tear to the glass eye thinking about it too much. Best not to think about it too much. Let's move right along.

Source videos: Cricket Australia, Cricket South Africa and England & Wales Cricket Board

Ozzy Man Reviews
MAN VS CHAIR
Released: 7 June 2017 on YouTube and Facebook

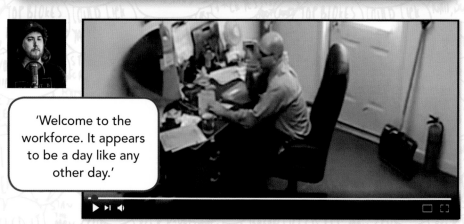

'Welcome to the workforce. It appears to be a day like any other day.'

'Oh no, this fella seems to have an issue with a piece-of-shit office chair provided by the manager.'

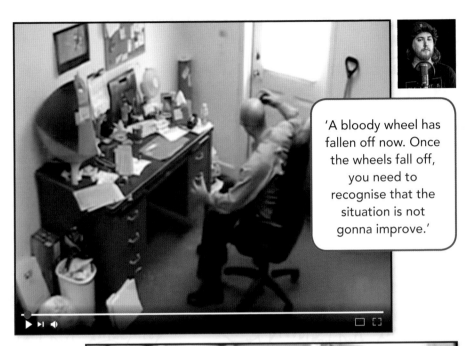

'A bloody wheel has fallen off now. Once the wheels fall off, you need to recognise that the situation is not gonna improve.'

'He fucken soldiers on, sits down and the chair throws him off! That was a beautiful takedown by the chair.'

'Unfortunately, the chair now has to feel the full wrath of the human!'

'Anyway, he's like "Fuck this place" and he does a walkout. Time to get an outdoors job.'

OZZY MAN REFLECTS ...

I try to keep a lookout for the obscure videos that people submit to the Ozzy Man Facebook or Gmail inboxes. I will generally listen to people when 500 of 'em send me the same video, but it's also important to listen to the softer voices of the few from time to time. This video was only submitted to me once. I love the rising action, it builds and builds and builds, and that's bloody fun to write commentary for. I couldn't tell ya if it was staged or fake, to be honest. I haven't been able to find out definitively. Anyhow, due to the sheer volume of messages sent to me these days, there are a lot of videos I simply don't see—but I'm glad I clicked on this one. A bloke fighting with an inanimate object is inherently funny.

I reckon it's a relatable video, too. Fuck, I've lost my temper at a chair before. I basically use chairs until they deteriorate and give me spinal problems. I once went to a chiropractor who told me to buy a better chair and stop sitting down so much. That's embarrassing as fuck. There's at least some dignity or manliness to having back problems from manual labour, but having a chiropractor tell you that you have back problems from sitting too much is a shameful moment, to say the least.

I've only ever had one office job! I lasted two years. I'm proud as punch with that. Other jobs I've had: *Community News* (delivering newspapers, in 1998—I got fired for dumping them), McDonalds, Blockbuster Video, Planet Video, Walkabout Bar (yep, over in England), Hyde Park Bottleshop, Kooyong Industrial Supplies (courier), Constable Care, Bogan Bingo, and a Balmoral hotel (pub quiz host). That's my résumé before Ozzy Man Reviews. RIP, video stores.

GLOSSARY OF AUSTRALIAN WORDS AND PHRASES

This list does not claim to cover all of the Aussie slang words and phrases that are known to man; there are loads of words and phrases that Australians have pulled out of their arses over the years. This list will cover the essentials and my personal favourites. You'll hear a bunch of these words and phrases in Ozzy Man videos or see 'em in the comment sections. Some of these words may cross over to other English-speaking countries, so you'll hear them in other places. Not all of 'em, but some of 'em. Our language and our accents are bastardised. We admit it. It doesn't faze us.

Acca Dacca   the legendary rock band AC/DC

agro   aggressive: 'Daz gets a bit agro when he's had a drink.' Agro was also the name of a puppet on Australian TV in the nineties. His show was called *Agro's Cartoon Connection*.

ambo   ambulance; also the paramedic driving the ambulance

ankle-biter   toddler, small human

arse   bum, butt, backside. Aussies prefer this spelling to 'ass' (we know that's a donkey).

arvo   afternoon

Aussie   person from Australia—I hope you already knew this one.

barbie   barbecue

bastard   a term of endearment: 'He's a good bastard.'

battler   someone who works hard to get by and survive: 'Tommo is an Aussie battler.'

beaut, bewdy   top quality: 'How's the beer, Bazza?' 'Bewdy, mate.'

biccy   biscuit: 'Fancy a couple of biccies with ya cuppa?'

big fuck-off (insert noun) describes an unusually large item, object or being. 'Mmm, you guys stay here, I'm gonna get one of those big fuck-off kebabs from across the road.'

bloke   man

bloody   an expletive used for emphasis; also common in British English: 'Bloody hell!' 'Bloody awesome!'

bloody oath   'I'm dead serious; this is no joke.'

bludger   lazy person: 'Get back to work, ya bludger!'

blue   fight, argument: 'They're havin' a blue next door. Listen to 'em.'

bog roll   toilet paper

bogan   someone a rich person looks down on. Your typical bogan sports a singlet, mullet, tattoos and footy shorts. Some bogans are dickheads, some are legends. Just like rich people.

bonza   brilliant

boofhead   idiot, fool

boogie board   small surfboard, body board. The bag of a boogie board can also be used to smuggle weed into Indonesia. Just be prepared to go to jail.

bottle-o   liquor store

Bradbury, doing a   a term derived from the Olympic medal race in which Australian ice skater Steve Bradbury meandered at the back of the pack until all the frontrunners stacked it (fell over), and he skated past and took gold. To do a Bradbury is to win at something in a remarkable way. Maybe you planned it; maybe you didn't—that's the genius of 'doing' or 'chucking' a Bradbury.

brekkie   breakfast

budgie smugglers   tight-fitting male swimwear, e.g. Speedos. Popular among men aged 50 and over. Former Australian prime minister Tony Abbott was famous for wearing his budgie smugglers at the beach with total pride.

bugger   an exclamation of surprise or discontent: 'Bugger me, that's amazing!' 'Bugger! I stubbed my fucken toe!'

bugger off   'Go away.'

Bundy   Bundaberg rum (made in Bundaberg, Queensland)

bush   forest, outback, rural countryside

BYO stands for Bring Your Own (alcohol). Many Australian party hosts do not provide alcohol, unless it's a milestone event like a 21st birthday or a wedding. When you see BYO on an invitation, it means you have to sort your own beverages out and choose what ya wanna drink. It's up to you whether you find this custom burdensome or liberating. Even if the party host wins Lotto and can afford to provide for everyone at the party, he'll probably still write 'Yeah nah BYO'.

cactus dead or dying: 'He's cactus, that bloke.'

Capper to take a mark in the style of Warwick Capper in Australian Rules football—you jump high and climb on someone's shoulders to catch the ball. It helps to yell 'CAPPEEEEERRRR!' like you're a hero, even if ya fuck it up and don't get anywhere near the ball.

carry on like a pork chop complain, ramble, exaggerate an issue

Centrelink Welfare

cheers! 'Thanks, mate, now let's drink.'

choccy chocolate

chockers, chockablock very full, no more room

choice the best, excellent: 'This mid-strength beer is choice.'

chook chicken

chook raffle a raffle (usually held in a pub) in which the prize is a chicken

chunder vomit

ciggie cigarette

cobber friend

come the raw prawn to attempt to deceive, lie: 'Don't come the raw prawn with me, mate, I know you're watering my beer down!'

coppa, copper police officer

corker great, excellent: 'What a corker!'

cranky pants in a bad mood, in a stinky

crikey an expression of surprise: 'Crikey! That is a bewdy of a crocodile.'

crock of shit nonsense, lies

crook sick, unwell, ill

cruising for a bruising if you keep behaving in the way you are, you're gonna get beaten up. A common saying among Australian Rules Under 12s coaches, used to retain order and discipline in the team: 'Daniel, quit mucking around! You're cruising for a bruising.' Now that I think about it, this usage is pretty abusive.

cunt person. This term isn't gender-specific in Australia, but don't be fooled into thinking we're amazingly progressive. Context and pre-established relationships are very important when it comes to this word. A 'shit cunt' can mean the worst kind of person, while a 'top cunt' means the best kind of person. Overall, it's true that the word is malleable in Australia, but it can definitely still be derogatory. Between good friends it is affectionate and a compliment.

cuppa a cup of tea

dack to pull someone's pants down. Usually a sibling's pants. 'MUUUUM, I got dacked!'

dag unfashionable person. The term is derived from the sheep-shearing industry, where 'dag' refers to the dried-up faeces that gets tangled in the wool around a sheep's butt. 'Todd, that shirt is daggy as fuck, mate.'

darl darling

deadly Indigenous slang for awesome, great, excellent

deadset without a doubt: 'That new area manager is a deadset fuckwit.'

defo definitely

destination fucked a term coined by Ozzy Man in the video where Australian Rules footballer Stefan Martin gets shirtfronted and knocked out. It indicates suffering a severe injury, or ending up in a circumstance that is very undesirable.

devo devastated: 'I'm devo that I missed out on the Acca Dacca concert.'

dickhead idiot, fool, dumbarse, bad person

didge didgeridoo (an Indigenous musical instrument)

digger soldier, member of the Australian army. This term was in common use towards the end of World War I.

dingo a wild dog found in the Australian outback

dob to tell on someone, to dob them in: 'Chad dobbed on me. He's a dobber.'

dog's breakfast a real mess: 'He made a fucken dog's breakfast of that one.'

dole see Centrelink: 'I'll go on the dole for a while till I sort my shit out.' 'Don't become a dole bludger.'

donga temporary transportable housing. Mining sites often have dongas for their workers.

donger penis

don't argue a fend, a block with a stiff arm: 'He's given that would-be tackler a don't argue!'

doof doof techno music

doona duvet, comforter, quilt

down under Australia. Yep, the whole thing.

drongo idiot, fool, dumbarse: 'What a bloody drongo.'

dunny toilet

durry cigarette

esky cooler for storing your beer in

fair dinkum one hundred per cent genuine, honest, truthful. 'Dinky-di' is a variation.

fair go giving someone a chance. Whether you like it or not, everyone deserves a fair go (unless you're positive he or she is a dead-set shit cunt).

fancy pants affluent, wealthy, classy: 'This is a fancy pants new home you got here, mate.'

feral someone who acts like they're living out in the wild: 'Clean up. You're feral!'

flamin' used as an enhancer: 'Get off the road, ya flamin' drongo!'

flanno flannelette shirt

flog a term previously used in regards to theft: 'He flogged a pack of ciggies from the deli.' However, it's now very much used as an insult, referring to someone who is full of shit, up themselves and arrogant: 'He's an absolute flog.' In some circles the word has become grossly over-used, and a great irony is forming in which the word 'flog' is getting dished out by people who sound like flogs themselves. The word doesn't have the precision and playfulness of galah, drongo or boofhead. It's a smidgen heavier than those old-fashioned slang words (but that's just like, you know, my opinion, man).

footy football; usually refers to Australian Rules football or rugby league

Foster's a beer from Australia that no one drinks, so it gets exported to England

Foster's flop a condition that occurs when you drink too much beer and it causes your penis to remain floppy, usually during a crucial moment when hardness is essential. 'She was ready to go, but I fucked it up. I was way too drunk. I got Foster's flop and just passed out.' Many one-night stands have quickly deteriorated due to the dreaded Foster's flop. There's not a single charity or support group out there to comfort blokes who self-sabotaged a great root. Realistically, getting a second go with the same woman is unlikely after a bout of Foster's flop. Don't keep texting her.

Foxtel Australia's national (over-priced) pay-TV company

Foxtel Now Foxtel's streaming service, which has become quite good but is still grossly over-priced

franger condom

fruit loop idiot, fool, dumbarse

fuck a duck! an expression of disappointment, frustration or anger

fuck all not many, if any

fuck me dead! an expression used when you're pleasantly surprised or frustrated or angry, as for 'fuck a duck'.

fuck me sideways! as above

fuck me silly! as above

fuck me stupid! as above

fuck me (ah bugger it, insert whatever word you like)! as above

fucked if I know an expression indicating uncertainty

fucken oath the same as bloody oath

galah idiot, fool, dumbarse: 'Haha, you're a galah!' 'They're a pack of galahs, the current cricket team.' Derived from the parrot-like bird.

gander have a look: 'Let's go down to the pork festival and have a gander; see what it's all about.'

g'day hello

geez unbelievable, unfathomable: 'Geeeez, no way!' Possibly derives from that Jesus bloke: 'Geezus!'

gives me the shits causes a great level of annoyance: 'He gives me the shits going on about his new Holden all the time.' Emphasis can be given by adding the word 'royal': 'He gives me the royal shits.'

gobby blow job

gone troppo a form of madness brought on by tropical weather: 'The humidity in Darwin can make ya go troppo.'

goon cheap cask wine: 'I shouldn't have drunk all that goon last night.'

goss gossip: 'What's the goss?'

grog alcohol

grouse wonderful, fantastic, great

gutful, had a fed up: 'I've had a fucken gutful of this bullshit. I'm going home.'

hard yakka hard work

Harold Holt a former Australian prime minister who went for a swim and vanished. To 'do a Harold Holt' or 'chuck a Harold Holt' means to fuck off without telling anyone and not return.

have a go, ya mug! an expression that combines encouragement and derision, usually heard at sporting events when one's team isn't being particularly inventive or risky. They're playing it too safe.

have a good one! enthusiastic regards: 'All the best!', 'Enjoy!'

Hiroshima facial a term coined by Ozzy Man's best mate, Mozza, describing a violent injury to the face. This is an explosive injury; expect a lot of blood coming from the nose or thereabouts.

HJ's Hungry Jack's. It's like Burger King.

hoon hooligan, one who speeds around quiet suburban streets doing burnouts

I wouldn't piss on him if he was on fire indicates a dislike for someone. You would not offer to help him out, even in a dire and desperate circumstance.

iffy dodgy, suspicious

joey baby kangaroo

Kiwi New Zealander

knock to criticise: 'Oi, don't knock it till ya try it.'

knock ya block off to punch someone so hard their head falls off

knuckle sandwich a punch

larrikin a mischievous and rowdy (but ultimately good-hearted) person: 'Quit dancing on the table, ya bloody larrikin.' A larrikin can still have some level of smarts, even if they act dumb. Not the same as a drongo or a galah or a boofhead or a dickhead or a flog.

longneck a 750 ml bottle of beer; also known as a king brown

Macca's McDonald's

mad as a cut snake crazy or angry

marvellous effort   when someone performs really well or does a great job: 'Marvellous effort, that.' It needs to be delivered in the accent of former cricket player and legendary commentator Richie Benaud.

mate   primarily means 'friend' but can be broadened to refer to anyone: 'Mate, fucken go! It's been green for ages!' The word can also be lengthened to express a whole range of emotions, from surprise to disappointment. Just stretch out the letter 'a': 'Maaaaaaaaate!'

mates' rates   when you get something cheaper than usual because you're a friend of the supplier

mint   great, excellent, the best

mintox   variation of 'mint' for extra emphasis. No idea who pulled this outta their arse. It was popular when I was in high school in 1999.

missus   someone's wife: 'How's the missus, mate?'

mob   group, tribe, entourage; not necessarily a bad or troublesome one: 'We'll head to the game at two p.m. and meet up with your mob after let's saaaay, six-ish?' Indigenous Australians will refer to their family and kin as their mob.

mozzie   mosquito

mull   marijuana

muso   musician: 'John Butler is a fair dinkum solid-as-fuck muso.'

muster   to gather up, to summon. Derived from rounding up sheep or cattle: 'I'll come out tonight if I can muster the energy.'

no worries   indicates agreement: 'No problem', 'Too easy', 'No drama'

no wucken furries   variation of 'No worries'

no wukkas   as above

nud, nuddy   naked: 'Oh, you forgot bathers (swimwear)? Just go in the nuddy.' To be clear, swimming naked in a friend's pool is not a social norm. A good reply would be: 'That's gross and embarrassing. It's not that hot anyway. I'm fine. Plus, you have air con. I'll stay near the air con.'

ocker   a rough-as-fuck Aussie who speaks in a broad accent; this term may be associated with bogans

onya   an expression of support, as in 'Good on you.'

outback   the vast, remote, glorious interior of Australia

pash   kiss. Note that a peck is without tongue, whereas a pash will usually involve some tongue action.

pash rash   red, irritated skin that forms as the result of a particularly intense pashing session. Common in teenagers and young adults. 'Look at your pash rash, Tash! Your face has been sandpapered!'

pav   pavlova. A controversial dessert, mainly because the bloody Kiwis keep trying to take credit for its invention. 'Pav' may also refer to Matthew Pavlich, a former Australian Rules footballer: 'Pav has plugged another goal!'

pig's arse   an expression of disbelief

pinga   Ecstasy tablet. Pingas are typically used to enhance the experience of sweaty summer 'doof doof' music festivals. Both the festival-goers and the coppas have been known to pop a pinga to get through the long day.

piss   alcohol (piss can refer to urine too, of course, but mostly means alcohol)

pissed   drunk ('maggoted', 'hammered' and 'legless' also fall under the umbrella of pissed)

polly   politician

Pom, Pommie   informal term for an Englishman. Not so much meant as an insult.

prang   collision, car accident; not usually a bad one—just one that leaves an annoying dent

prezzie   present, gift

pub   bar

pull the wool over your eyes   to act deceitfully, to trick you, to lie to you

punter   paying customer: 'The punters were furious when Foxtel's live stream crashed.'

Radelaide   Adelaide. An attempt to make it sound great, like it's a 'rad' place. Points for effort.

ratbag   troublemaker; usually in reference to kids or youth

rellie   relative, member of the extended family: 'The rellies are coming round for Chrissie (Christmas).'

ridgy-didge   good, genuine, original. May be derived from a term for ridged gold coins.

ripper   excellent, beauty, magnificent: 'You little ripper!'

ripsnorter   variation of 'ripper'

roadie   takeaway alcohol: 'Grab a couple of roadies before we leave (the pub or house).'

roo   kangaroo

root   sexual intercourse

rug up   to put on extra clothes when it's cold outside: 'Gotta rug up when we go to the dam to catch some marron (a freshwater crayfish) tonight.'

scab   to beg, to try to get something for free: 'See if you can scab a dollar off Liz to get a Choc Chill.'

schooner   an awkward-sized glass of beer that some pubs offer to punters. Your mate may think it's responsible and socially acceptable to order a schooner because it's not as big as a pint and it doesn't look as soft as a middy (mid-sized glass, half-pint). The schooner is an over-conscientious middle ground.

scratchies   scratch lottery tickets: 'That drongo spends half his Centrelink money on fucken scratchies. Won fifty bucks once and reckons "the big one" is just around the corner.'

scull   to drink fast, to down ya beer. We may've stolen that from the Vikings, who would say 'Skol' as a toast.

servo   petrol station

sheep shagger   New Zealander (we love 'em really, though: they're a bunch of top cunts!)

sheila   woman

she'll be right   it'll be okay, nothing bad will happen

shit stirrer   jokester, prankster, smart-arse

shithouse   really bad: 'I've had a shithouse day.' Derived from the outdoor dunny.

shitmixed   hurt, injured, hit hard by something or someone

shonky   poorly done. Current affairs programmes on Australian TV usually like to expose shonky home builders and shonky retail businesses.

shotgun!   something you yell when ya wanna sit in the front passenger seat and the car's filling up with a few folks. A variation on 'bagz': 'Shut up, I already bagzed it!'

show pony   someone who tries too hard

sickie   taking a sick day. A sickie is fine, but 'chucking a sickie' means you're probably faking it.

sink some piss   consume a decent quantity of alcohol

slab   a 24-pack of beer: 'That fucken maniac reckons he'll polish off the entire slab tonight!'

smoko   short break, usually to smoke a durry

snag, snagga sausage: 'Chuck a few more snags on the barbie.'

snazzy fancy

soft cock lacking strength of character

sook sulk, cry, whine

spewin' very angry or devastated: 'I'm spewin' I missed out on the all-you-can-eat buffalo wings!'

spiffy of high quality

spready spreading one's legs, doing the splits

spunk good-looking person (defo don't use that term in the UK: it means 'jizz' over there)

squizz to have a look, to have a gander

sticky beak similar to 'squizz' and 'gander', but with a nosier connotation. 'Quit sticky beaking, just leave 'em alone.'

stiffy erection

stitch up to trick someone, to prank 'em, to embarrass 'em: 'Mick got stitched up beautifully the other day.'

Straya Australia

strewth! an exclamation of disbelief or shock

stubby bottle of beer

stubby holder insulated sleeve into which a beer can/bottle is inserted to keep cool during the heat of an Australian summer's day. Known as a beer cooler or koozy in Britain and North America.

sunnies sunglasses

ta thank you

take the piss to make fun of, to stir someone up, to jest. Basically Ozzy Man's whole career is built on taking the piss.

tall poppy successful person

tall poppy syndrome a condition in which the sufferer tends to overly criticise or dislike successful people. Spraying Heath Ledger with a water gun at a media event was the action of a journalist with tall poppy syndrome.

thingo a useful replacement for any word you can't remember: 'Pass us that thingo.'

thongs flip-flops

tinnie can of beer

togs swimwear

too right! indicates enthusiastic agreement: 'Definitely!'

tosser   idiot, fool, dumbarse; especially someone who is full of himself or loves himself too much. Derived from the act of masturbation. One could speculate that the latest Australian buzzword 'flog' is a mutation of 'tosser'.

trackies   tracksuit pants; you can also say 'trackie dacks'. Nothing beats a day on the couch doing fuck all in ya trackie dacks.

tradie   tradesman. Specific types of tradies include the brickie (bricklayer), truckie (truck driver), sparky (electrician), poo man (plumber), garbo (rubbish collector) and chippie (carpenter).

true blue   genuine, the real deal

tucker   food

Ugg boots   warm sheepskin footwear. These are not slippers—they're WAY better than slippers. Uggs are up there with Vegemite and Tim Tams when it comes to homegrown brands and products that Australians are proud of.

undies   underwear

up the duff   pregnant. Fucked if I know who made that one up.

ute   utility vehicle, pickup truck

veg out   to sit on the couch and watch TV without doing too much critical thinking

walkabout   to go walkabout is to travel nationally or internationally, or even to wander and get lost locally. Derived from Indigenous rites of passage.

wanker   idiot, fool, dumbarse, someone who is full of himself

whinge   whine: 'Nana's having a whinge coz she wants to watch *Coronation Street* and we keep flicking it over to the footy.'

whopper   gigantic, humungous. Also the name of a burger at Hungry Jack's.

wobbly   temper tantrum: 'She chucked a wobbly.'

wog   informal term for a person of Mediterranean descent. Not so much meant as an insult.

woody   erection, stiffy

woop woop   the middle of nowhere: 'He's living out in woop woop now.'

wuss   coward

ya reckon?   'Is that what you think?' Can be used sarcastically and ironically, in response to statements like 'Don't jump out of the plane until your parachute is on.' 'Ohhhh, ya reckon? Fuck, I was just about to jump, eh.'

yak   to vomit: 'I think I yakked last night. Dunno for sure though. Tastes like it I reckon.'

Yank   informal term for an American. Not so much meant as an insult. Some Australians will use 'Seppo' if they wish to be derogatory to an American. That one is derived from rhyming 'septic tank' with 'Yank'—it implies that an American is full of shit, like a septic tank. It can be meant as banter and said with affection, but the underlying connection to poo can understandably hurt a Yank's feelings. It's one of those tough ones that's in a bit of a grey area.

yeah nah   the speaker's tone is key here. Sometimes 'Yeah . . . nah' is a shutdown, a disagreement. In a different context it may be used as a filler, to bide your time until you can confirm yes or no with confidence: 'Yeah nah nah nah nah, ohhh yeah, nah, nah, nup. Yeah, okay, aw nah, nah, nah.' It can also mean yes if you say it quickly: 'Yeah nah no worries. Let's do it.' The term is extremely flexible when you truly break it down.

yobbo   an uncultured, uncouth person. A yobbo is similar to a bogan but a different breed. Some people may get lumped into the category of bogan purely due to their socio-economic standing or their choice of suburb to live in. A yobbo, in contrast, is likely to be identified on a behavioural level only.

you're dreamin'   'You're being unrealistic; it's never going to happen.' A classic saying, popularised further by the Australian movie *The Castle*. When someone is attempting to sell a second-hand item at a high price, you need to say 'Tell him he's dreamin'!'

SOURCE VIDEO CREDITS

Ozzy Man Reviews: Ice-bucket Challenge Fails
Source videos, from start of section:
(1) The Besties Show, Nicole Marie Johnson and Carrie Finkley; (2) Sofie Tollefson and Jukin Video; (3) John Deluca and Collab Clips; (4) source unknown; (5) Launchpad Screeners; (6, 7) Grady Riley and Jukin Video

Ozzy Man Reviews: Nicki Minaj, 'Anaconda'
Source video: NickiMinajAtVevo

Ozzy Man Reviews: WTF Happened in March 2015
Source videos, from start of section:
(1) Jukin Video; (2, 3) Storyful and Ashton Webster; (4) Tim Dinte, YouTube; (5) Mediaworks and Fremantle Media; (6) Claus Jorgensen, YouTube; (7) Jukin Video; (8) bhminden, YouTube; (9) National Geographic

Ozzy Man Reviews: *Game of Thrones* Season 6, Ep 9
Source video: HBO

Ozzy Man Reviews: Yanet García and Mexican Weather
Source video: Televisa Monterrey and iamYanetGarcia, YouTube

Ozzy Man & Mozza Commentate: A Kangaroo Street Fight
Source video: ViralHog

Ozzy Man Reviews: Cows vs Turtle
Source video: Jukin Video

Ozzy Man Reviews: Men's Diving
Source video: 28th SEA Games Singapore and Sport Singapore, YouTube

Ozzy Man Reviews: Bunny vs Dogs
Source video: Run Rabbit Run, Liveleak (original videographer unknown)

Ozzy Man Reviews: Stereosonic
Source video: Stereosonic Exposed, Facebook

Ozzy Man Reviews: Duck vs Tiger
Source video: Symbio Wildlife Park NSW

Ozzy Man Reviews: AFL vs Soccer Big Hit
Source video: Australian Football League and Danish Football Association

Ozzy Man Reviews: An Octopus Eating a Crab
Source video: ViralHog

Ozzy Man Reviews: Funniest Kickboxing Match Ever
Source video: Broadcasting Services of Thailand, Chong sib-ed (Channel 11)

Ozzy Man Reviews: Grandpa vs Brown Snake
Source video: Jukin Video

Ozzy Man Reviews: Indecisive Lioness Hunting
Source video: Jukin Video

Ozzy Man Reviews: Mantis vs Cat
Source video: André Regius, YouTube

Ozzy Man Reviews: Rio Olympics Highlights #1
Source video: International Olympic Committee

Ozzy Man & Mozza Commentate: Bunny vs Snake
Source video: Momma Rabbit, YouTube

Ozzy Man Reviews: Clowns
Source videos, from start of section:
(1) CBS Chicago and Brad Graham, YouTube; (2) Leaferbag, YouTube; (3) News4Jax; (4) HelloGum, YouTube; (5) Rangel Photography (SSR)

Ozzy Man Reviews: People Fucked Up by Bulls
Source video: Gabriel Alves Vieira (fotogabriel), YouTube

Ozzy Man Reviews: Iguana vs Snakes (*BBC's Planet Earth II*)
Source video: BBC Earth

Ozzy Man Reviews: Beer Deaths
Source videos, from start of section:
(1) hutzelbrot8888, YouTube; (2) Dude Stuff, YouTube; (3) Mirko Blanks, YouTube; (4) HD Broadcaster (Paul Szott), YouTube; (5) Phinel Sul de Minas

Ozzy Man Reviews: Mick Fanning vs Shark
Source video: World Surf League

Ozzy Man Reviews: Irish Bouncer vs Drunkards
Source video: ViralHog

Ozzy Man Reviews: Greatest Olympic Win Ever
Source video: International Olympic Committee

Ozzy Man Reviews: MMA 9-second Knockout
Source video: Super Fight League, India

Ozzy Man Reviews: Crow vs Cat vs Cat
Source video: will20091995, YouTube

Ozzy Man Reviews: Cricket Nut Shots
Source videos: Cricket Australia, Cricket South Africa and England & Wales Cricket Board

Ozzy Man Reviews: Man vs Chair
Source video: source unknown

ABOUT THE AUTHOR

Ethan Marrell launched Ozzy Man Reviews on YouTube and Facebook in April 2014. He remembers it like it was yesterday. He was watching *Game of Thrones* Season 4 and wanted to talk to someone about all the shit that was going down in the show (Jaime and Cersei were pissing him off). Having previously dabbled in filmmaking, screenwriting, stand-up comedy and hosting Bogan Bingo, and with the name 'Ozzy Man' fresh in his head after visiting some American friends who called him that, he thought it would be a cool idea to put a decade's worth of creative ventures into a turbo-powered blender and have a gander at what came out.

What did come out was a recap and review of *Game of Thrones* Season 4, Episode 3, 'Breaker of Chains'. The key creative thought during the experimental process was to make sure the video editing, writing and final voice-over felt like being at a raucous party. The video was uploaded to the web, and *Game of Thrones* fans showed up and commented that Ozzy Man needed to make videos every week, so he made *GoT* videos every week. Then, in the off season, he found other shit to do to keep the YouTube channel and Facebook page alive.

You wouldn't know it to look at him, but Ozzy Man is an academic dickhead. He studied at Curtin University in Perth from 2013 to 2015 and has a master's degree in Internet Communications. Grinding out essays on web media and social networks definitely helped the birthing of Ozzy Man Reviews. Despite performance influences such as The Eric Bana Sketch Show series, The Twelfth Man, Roy & HG, *Crocodile Dundee* and the legend Steve Irwin, there were also some big-time academic influences on Ozzy Man—Lawrence Lessig and Henry Jenkins are the two that come immediately to mind.

The wanker was born on 2 February 1986, so that makes him 31 years old at the time of writing this. He doesn't have long-term goals, but he does have some savings and a wife. That's good shit.

FUCK YES, YA BOOK-READING WANKER, FUCK YES!

Thanks to Regan Roberts, Amir, Sadaf, and all me family and friends.